A M B E

MW01613037

FIGHTING THE GOOD FIGHT OF FAITH WITH YOUR CHILD IN PUBLIC SCHOOL

Fighting the Good Fight of Faith with Your Child in Public School
Trilogy Christian Publishers
A Wholly Owned Subsidiary of Trinity Broadcasting Network
2442 Michelle Drive
Tustin, CA 92780

For information, address Trilogy Christian Publishing
Rights Department, 2442 Michelle Drive, Tustin, Ca 92780.
Trilogy Christian Publishing/ TBN and colophon are trademarks of Trinity Broadcasting Network.
For information about special discounts for bulk purchases, please contact Trilogy Christian Publishing.
Manufactured in the United States of America
Trilogy Disclaimer: The views and content expressed in this book are those of the author and may not necessarily reflect the views and doctrine of Trilogy Christian Publishing or the Trinity Broadcasting Network.
10 9 8 7 6 5 4 3 2 1
Library of Congress Cataloging-in-Publication Data is available.
ISBN: 979-8-88738-675-1
ISBN: 979-8-88738-676-8

DEDICATION

I dedicate this book to my Lord and Savior Jesus Christ, to my loving husband and three children, all of whom make this book possible.

Dare to dream

TABLE OF CONTENTS

Chapter 1: My Awakening of the Faith. 7

Chapter 2: Survival. 13

Chapter 3: Child Disciples 19

Chapter 4: Growing the Faith. 29

Chapter 5: Teach the Faith 37

Chapter 6: Being Salt and Light 47

Chapter 7: Practice Fighting the Good Fight 53

Chapter 8: Parents Lead 61

Chapter 9: You Are Never Alone 71

Chapter 10: How It All Began 79

Basics on How to Lead a Study 87

Thoughts for Leaders 89

Fighting the Good Fight of Faith
with Your Child in Public School 90

CHAPTER 1

MY AWAKENING OF THE FAITH

"Fight the good fight of the faith. Take hold of the eternal life to which you were called when you made your good confession in the presence of many witnesses." 1 Timothy 6:12 (NIV)

Gladiator. When a gladiator enters the arena, he is ready to fight. He has trained. He has his armor for protection and his sword to take down his opponent. He has all he needs for victory. Or does he? He also needs the will to fight! Before we go into an arena, we need to gather the tools needed for victory. God gives us everything we need to train for this in scripture. We must choose for ourselves to take hold of the eternal life where God has called us. God doesn't want us to struggle in the arena for no good reason but to serve His Kingdom to further His plans. He promises to come through when we walk in obedience. Public school is our arena. We are in training and God is bringing the victories!

> *"And without faith it is impossible to please God, because anyone who comes to him must believe that he exists and that he rewards those who earnestly seek him." Hebrews 11:6 (NIV)*

Indeed, He came for the lost. I once was lost, and He came for his lost sheep-me! I knew God would teach me how to be a mom, because I had no idea what that looked like. My mother had died when I was young and most of my life, she struggled with alcohol abuse. She also endured many years of physical abuse from my stepdad that I witnessed. I love and miss her very much, but she could never break free of that addiction. She found freedom at the end with Jesus. So, you see, I needed all the help I could get from the Lord. How did I do that exactly?

Scripture says, ask and you shall receive. All my help has come from God and seeking Him out in prayer, reading my Bible, and applying what I was learning.

One of the most important years for our family was 2011. Cory, my husband, and I began to pray daily and fast a couple days a week in August. We were praying and believing we would gain the funds to tour Israel with a group from our church in 2012. It would be a miracle, as we didn't have one dollar to save in our budget. My aunt works with mortgages, and in September she called to let us know that interest rates had dropped quite a bit, and it may be a good idea to refinance our house. She also said we may be able to get some cash out to help with our van that kept breaking down. Cory said it was from the Lord, so we refinanced. By October, we received a check in the mail that was the exact amount it cost for both of us to go to Israel! And our house payment was still lower. Miracle! This was just the beginning of many more miracles to come. We traveled to Israel in July of 2012. Israel changed everything for us. It was during this trip that my faith grew more than ever before. Of course, my faith had grown at different times of my life, but this was different. The experience awakened us in so many ways.

One of the ways that it changed was the way we read our Bibles. We had visited this place that is full of history, and now we could visualize the stories of the Bible and the places came to life.

Excavations were uncovering the history of where events happened around every corner, and they are still uncovering biblical sites to this day. Science keeps pointing towards this important life book of history!

I never knew about all the evidence that supports the Bible, and it was truly amazing to be a part of such an eye-opening experience. I have been a believer since I was a teenager, but God unfolded mysteries in those moments. I am so thankful. I could probably write a whole book about my travels to Israel!

I brought back an urgency to share my experiences there and teach my children how important every single person is in this world. We are here to love people fiercely and live out our faith with others daily, even if they don't know Jesus yet. It's simple even though sometimes we make things harder than they need to be. God loves people; we just need to love people, too.

I have often wondered what my purpose in life would be. I prayed so much these days and asked God, "What is my purpose for you?" I would tell Him many times that I wanted to bring the lost to Him, and to serve Him all my days.

I had the wonderful opportunity to lead a group for moms at my church, even though I never felt qualified. It was one of my favorite times in my life. I made many friends, and that was so important to me. When I was younger, we bounced around homes so much that I was never able to keep friends for very long before we moved again. I cherish that time with those ladies: we learned so much together. I also had three small children at the time and God confirmed to me, what seems like forever ago, that my purpose was to build a foundation rooted in scripture and teach my children about Jesus.

God called me out of the ministry with the mom's group, audibly. I wasn't sure why at the time and I must admit I was angry at God for calling me out of a group of people I loved so much. I spent my last summer there before leaving in August with no plans for my next step. I needed to wait on God. I cried and mourned that season. There had been an urgency on my heart for quite a while. I did not know what my next steps were for a couple months, but that urgency was getting stronger and stronger, and I realized, finally, at the end of those months what I was supposed to do! The message kept coming to help other families with children in public schools. I loved and respected the women I had ministered with and many of them had been led to home school their children to teach them with a Christian worldview. This was absolutely right for them as they had prayed and had been led by the Lord.

When Cory and I prayed for the path our children should take for school, God chose the path of public school for our children. We were excited about helping them and teaching them to navigate sharing their faith with the majority, where it is not a popular place to do so. As parents, at times, we felt very alone with a lack of support in fighting the good fight of faith in this place. But we believed that our children were the salt and light that others needed. Every place I looked, there was no help in a community-based atmosphere. In fact, God kept pushing me through scripture and I vented to Him often enough about this, until He showed me in scripture Matthew 9: 37-38 (NIV) *He said to God's disciples, "the harvest is plentiful, but the workers are few, ask the Lord of the harvest, therefore, to send out workers into His harvest field."* After reading that verse, I finally realized what God was telling me...... **I was the one to do something about it**.

The idea came for me to write something to help our community of families who have children in public school. I had been shown so much of my children's friends and the help that needed to happen. Many children are being raised by their grandparents, foster parents, single working parents, some who are homeless and in dire circumstances, others are hungry. We would be helping these families! I asked God, *am I strong enough?* Then I remembered the scripture: *"But he said to me, 'My grace is sufficient for you, for my power is made perfect in weakness.' Therefore, I will boast all the more gladly about my weaknesses, so that Christ's power may rest upon me."* 2 Corinthians 12:9 (NIV) For Jesus and those little ones, the least of these, I got to work and wrote a study that my husband and myself would lead. The study is for families with children K-12.

We led many groups over a period of seven years and counting, helping hundreds of families. God is good! What led me to write a book like this, adding to the six-week study, is to share all the hope from the amazing stories of our children's experiences in public school with everyone we can. Anyone with children in public schools can benefit from reading this book and can bring a group together to bring that hope to each other, by leading the attached study at the end. God knows who needs it; I pray He puts it in the hands of many in whom it will bless and encourage. The Bible says God loves David because "he will do everything I want him to do." This scripture has always impacted me because I want God to love me like that! I love my God. I will always do everything He asks me to do, which includes writing this book. God-this one's for you!

CHAPTER 2
SURVIVAL

The way my life began does not stand out as unusual in today's standards. Many have had harder circumstances that they've survived. God has used my life to help others that have experienced similar circumstances and is continuing to do so to this day through my family in many different ways, but mainly by fighting the good fight of faith in public schools alongside my children. In the beginning of my life, it was more like fighting the good fight of survival, not faith. The transformation changed later as I learned about what faith in God was. This is some of my story that shaped my perspective about public schools.

My parents divorced when I was three years old, and although my mom had custody of my little brother and me, she would leave me with my grandparents, especially when she was dating my stepdad. I was raised by my grandparents for some of my early childhood with frequent visits from my mom, every other weekend spent with my dad.

My stepdad entered my life when I was five. It was the beginning of something else hard in my life to accept and survive. Even though he seemed like a good partner for my mom to be happy and to gain a family setting, he was not the person he pretended to be in public. When he was sober, he was funny, outgoing, and very social, the life of every gathering. That soon faded as he began to drink and do drugs more often. Somehow, no one could see what was hiding underneath that facade. After they married, my mother moved me to the schools in Nashville and we lived with them. He would beat my mom brutally. I often thought she would die. She began drinking daily. I could see her pain, emotionally and physically. Often, she would cry uncontrollably, and I took on the role of taking care of her and cleaning up after her alcohol use. I would also help her up off the floor because she couldn't walk and take care of her after my stepdad would leave angrily after physically abusing her. We didn't find out until much later that she was battling mental health issues as well.

I was scared a lot, because my mom started drinking even while driving wherever we needed to go. There were a couple of times we fought about her drinking and driving. It made her angry and we would argue heavily because I was so scared; a couple of moments I remember her taking her hands off the wheel and sarcastically telling me to drive.

Chapter 2: Survival

We skidded off the road and almost wrecked both times. I stopped saying anything about it. I was always relieved when we arrived at our destination, wherever that was. Everywhere we lived was temporary housing, and every weekend she had us was spent traveling to their friends' places where I would sleep on a big "body pillow" that went with us. I don't remember feeling safe at any of those places. But I felt most safe while I was at school.

This is not to say there were no good memories of my mom. She was 4'11" and about ninety-five pounds. She was fun and playful when she was in a good mood. The metamorphosis to being unhealthy was a slow roll-out and very confusing for a child to witness. I loved my mother fiercely and wanted to remain loyal to her, no matter how badly she behaved. I was a casualty of divorce, never having a feeling of where I belonged. I remember not feeling like I was enough to keep a family together. Those feelings also came back while my mom struggled with her addictions. Why wasn't I enough of a good reason for her to get sober and leave this violent person? Yes, she tried many times but could not break free, like so many others.

I struggled with loneliness and insecurities, and I didn't know it at the time but also rejection. I had a lot of freedom throughout my childhood and spent most days while I was with my grandparents, outside picking blackberries or wandering through the woods in my grandmother's silky nightgowns pretending to be a little fairy Princess of the Woods. While with my mom and stepdad, I would spend my extra time after school outside playing, mostly in creeks that were close by to wherever we stayed at the time. I would search for lizards, frogs, crawdads, and snakes. We would also camp in tents in different areas, always near lakes. I swam in every river, creek and lake that was nearby. Being outside in nature was always a love of mine. It calmed me. I continued to create fantasies in my mind to escape whatever thoughts I did not want. There were good moments and bad moments; however, my child-like mind would fear the bad moments that would come, always expecting the sky to fall. I learned how to escape in my mind to think about fun things, happy things, and daydreaming became something familiar that I could lean on to feel better at times.

I would daydream often to keep me from feeling alone, even in a classroom setting. I thrived in my friendships at school but would move again, having to make new friends. While living in that nightmare with my mom and stepdad, I was scared constantly. School was a safe place for me, and my friends were what I had to get me through my worst days. I laughed with them, and they even took up for me in moments of being bullied. I felt protected by my friends. Some of them had hard circumstances too, but when we were together, we were stronger. I remember them welcoming me as the new girl, listening to the best of the 80's music, and teaching me the latest dance moves. In those moments, I was able to be myself and let any guards down.

In my mom's search for redemption and for the right church, we visited many different denominations, never settling on any. We visited Baptist, Methodist, Church of God (my Papa's church), Church of Christ (my grandmother's church), Episcopal and some non-denominational. I was often called a church gypsy by friends. This was also the case in my home life, always moving and never having any stability long term anywhere. What will I eat? Where will I sleep? I never knew and at times I remember being hungry. Mama never prioritized food like when I lived with my grandparents. We had a garden there and my grandmother cooked for us every day. I always looked forward to visiting my grandparents on the weekends. Little did I know, these hard times and events would influence my views and passions once I grew older and had a family of my own.

You may ask, "Where was your dad in all this?" He was there. Always. But in order to stay loyal to my broken and weak mother, I kept secrets from him. This created a huge rift in our relationship. The fact is he never missed a child support payment. He never failed to show up for our scheduled weekends. He just didn't know what he didn't know. He was doing his best, but every moment I was safe with him I wondered if my mother was also safe. Was she eating? Was she getting hurt? But my attitude came across as distant and ungrateful so we kind of battled. I am so grateful that I have been able to heal my relationship with my dad.

By the Grace of God, He called me, and I heard His voice. I sought Him and found a church home as a young adult. I somehow met the most wonderful man who became my husband and God blessed us with a beautiful family. God is Good!

CHAPTER 3
CHILD DISCIPLES

*"A new command I give to you: Love one
another. As I have loved you, so you must love one
another. By this everyone will know that you are my
disciples if you love one another."*
John 13:34-34 (NIV)

Helping your child learn to navigate public school is not an easy task, but it can be done. It takes constant awareness and can be overwhelming, at times, with all the information that comes our way. Here are some stories that can encourage you to fight the good fight of faith in your journey with your child in the public-school setting.

In August of 2012, my oldest began first grade and my middle child began Kindergarten Readiness. God reminded me that my children belonged to Him first; however, I continued to struggle with anxiety. I had this overwhelming fear that the foundation that we rooted our kids in would be erased in public school! I discussed my fear and anxiety with my husband, and we decided we would pray together and ask the Lord for help. Psalms 91 was scripture we had prayed in Israel, and it helped comfort me to speak these promises out loud. So, every morning on the car ride to school, I would give my oldest, who was six years old, the laminated card we carried in Israel with Psalms 91, and she would read it aloud until we got to school. One morning in October, she informed me that she didn't need the card any longer. She began to pray the Psalm and as she began, my middle and youngest started to recite it with her! My youngest was two and my middle was four at the time. (The two-year-old made me smile every time he said "pestilence," Pretty adorable.) I was overcome with joy and cried! It took me a few extra months to memorize, but it was helping all of us to say this special scripture for safety and security out loud on the way to school.

God was so good to teach us, and I realized that my anxiety was less and less every morning. Even as I celebrated these moments, I would continue to put God in a box, not believing completely that He would keep my kids safe. Lack of trust on my part stemming from what was screaming at me, my every insecurity and unsafe moment in my past life. Let's be honest, trusting the Lord is something easy to say but hard to actually do. So, in continuing to practice reciting the truth of scripture, I leaned on, "Trust in the Lord with all your heart, lean not on your own understanding; in all your

ways acknowledge Him and He shall direct your paths."
Proverbs 3:5-6 (NKJV)

As I was learning to be quicker in trusting the Lord
in all things involving my kids, He began to give me
opportunities to stand in what I believe, and to share with
others what I was applying in my life. It was renewing my
mind daily and confirming his promise that we, including
my children, could be in this world but not conform to the
pattern of this world.

> *"Do not conform to the pattern of this world
> but be transformed by the renewing of your
> mind. Then you will be able to test and approve
> what God's will is- his good, pleasing, and
> perfect will." Romans 12:2 (NIV).*

In October of 2012, my oldest was in first grade, and they
were discussing Halloween, which can be a fun subject
for little kids. She brought home a book that she checked
out from the school library that mentioned spells and
even contained a "spell." Since I knew it was something
I didn't want her to read, I instructed her to take it back
to the library the next day. She also talked about another
book they were reading together as a class. I explained to
her I would reach out to the teacher to request an alternate
assignment during the group reading time. I scheduled
an appointment with her teacher, and I was completely
unsure of anything I would say. I remember praying in
my van on the way to school and a Chris Tomlin song
came on, *God of Angel Armies*. I sang so loud (and not

well, I might add), but I gained strength on the way to the meeting.

I arrived at the classroom and sent my three little ones to play. I introduced myself and the teacher quickly asked me why my daughter couldn't read the books she checked out. Scripture immediately came to my mind, Philippians 4:8-9. I explained that we watch over what our children read and watch, simply gave that scripture as what we follow. The teacher's eyes filled with tears. She began to tell me that my child had shared her faith with every single child in her classroom.

She told me she knew about our trip to Israel, how we pray Psalm 91 every morning, and how we pray for all the teachers every morning. The teacher shared with me how my child had renewed her personal faith because she had never seen a child her age do what she has done. I was completely taken aback and shocked at what was happening. I was thinking, *my child is six years old*!

I don't remember leaving the classroom or the school, but somehow, I managed to leave with all three of my small children that day. I felt like I was walking out of a cloud! Did God really do that? Unbelievably, He wasn't even done! The library teacher emailed me later that day informing me that they were changing their series to read to the library class, too! I never asked for this; God moved! This was the day that I let God out of the box and was the beginning of more to come.

That same year, my middle child began Kindergarten

Readiness. I adored her teacher. My oldest had already been in her class. We prayed for her teacher and all the students. In the first few weeks of school, my child began talking about a little girl in her class who wasn't being nice to her. She would push her when they were lining up to go to music, lunch, or recess. She would also stick her tongue out at her, which really hurt my child's feelings. So, we prayed and asked God to help her at school. We came up with one sentence to say to this girl every time she would act out, "Jesus loves you, and I do, too."

It seemed like something small. My husband and I also had a conversation with our child explaining how many children have hard circumstances at home and being mean usually comes from a place of insecurity and not feeling good about yourself. She understood and kept repeating this one sentence daily. As time went by, things seemed to get better. I wanted my children to feel good and safe at school, but I knew there would be obstacles to help them overcome. What did we do together when an obstacle would come? We would pray, ask for the Lord's help and guidance.

We leaned on Him by reading scripture and communicating with our kids daily on how to live out what we were learning together.

Fast forward to a field trip, I was anxious to meet this little girl who was giving my child trouble. When my child pointed out who had been taunting her, I was shocked. I saw this tiny, spunky, and pretty little girl. She was glued to me and my child the entire field trip. The Bible says that we are a fragrance to some and to others a repellent. I realized in that moment, as she gravitated toward my child, that God was doing something with this unlikely friendship.

By the end of the year, this girl had changed her behavior toward my child, and they had somehow become friends. Over the years in elementary, I would come to volunteer at the school and this little girl would hug me in the hallway. She would smile so big when she saw me that my heart would jump in my chest. I had watched her get older and did not know her circumstances, until one day at the Fun Run at school. I was sitting with my middle child and this girl came to sit with us in the bleachers. I asked my child if she was happy I was there, and this little girl quickly chimed in, "I am!" I smiled and told her thank you. Then she said something I will never forget. She said, "I wish you were my mama." I was quiet for a moment, then asked, "Where is your mama?"

Our Conversation:

CHILD: "She's addicted to drugs; I haven't seen her since I was a baby."

ME: "Where's your daddy?"

CHILD: "In prison, I've never seen him."

ME: "Who is taking care of you?"

CHILD: "My Grandmother. It's just me and her."

ME: "Grandmothers are special. My grandparents raised me, too. I bet she takes good care of you. Does she take you to church?"

CHILD:" Yes, we go to church."

ME: "That's good. We need to know Jesus. He's my best friend. He is yours, too!"

She smiled so big at me; I could hardly contain the tears welling up in my eyes. We sat there and talked more, but I'll never forget that day. She and my daughter were called for the Fun Run soon after that. As I watched from the bleachers that day, I was amazed how God brought these sweet girls together. It was clear that this girl had experienced trauma and extreme loss in her life. It reminded me of a window of my childhood, being raised by my grandparents and being incredibly thankful for my friendships that I would cling to in my life at that time. Grandparents are not supposed to be raising their grandchildren, but that is the reality for so many children and very real. We have also encountered homeless children and plenty of other children living at poverty levels and in dire circumstances. Some are hungry and some are dealing with abuse in the home. Public school is their life- line, as well as churches and other organizations in the community that reach out to help these families. It is important! Struggles can come no matter the financial status, and circumstances can quickly change in any family.

We have intentionally pointed out these situations to

our children and have had many discussions on these subjects. This is life we are teaching them. We can have these important discussions with them and teach them how to seek out those children who are hurting while they are at school. "The King will reply, 'Truly I tell you, whatever you did for one of the least of these brothers and sisters of mine, you did for me.'" Matthew 25:40 (NIV)

What I have noticed is how God has sown tremendous empathy in my children because they have seen their friends go through all these things over the years since they were little. It is so important to communicate with your children and walk them through it and validate these moments of learning. I am so thankful I had friends of faith in my life in my younger years. I felt alone many moments and leaned on these friendships before I ever accepted the Lord in my life. I am so thankful I asked God what my children's purpose for Him in the very beginning of their lives would be! He answered. He has and is continuing to show continuously how He is saving and bringing precious children and families to know Him! Are you ready? You can have these opportunities too! Implement small things and they will grow to bigger things!

One of my favorite scriptures that the Lord has given me over the many years of overcoming is the one in Genesis. "As far as I am concerned, God turned into good what you meant for evil, for he brought me to this high position I have today so that I could save the lives of many people." Genesis 50:20 (TLB)

I have come across many scriptures exactly at the time needed while seeking answers through scripture. God has a purpose for your child as young as a toddler and elementary age as much as he does an older teenager in high school or college. Do not be discouraged if your child is in high school and you think it's too late. It is never too late to find your purpose or your child's purpose, no matter the age! If you think God is moving, stay tuned! If you think you are alone, you are not! While God is teaching us, we can share things we are learning with our child at their age, whatever the age. We can help our children develop their God stories, and it changes as they get older. Their stories of how God helps them in school and how they share their faith in the hard places is how they will grow. God will help your child share their God stories and bring others in to show each human their purpose no matter their ages! We have witnessed this personally with our family and others!

CHAPTER 4
GROWING THE FAITH

"Repent and be baptized, every one of you, in the name of Jesus Christ for the forgiveness of your sins. And you will receive the gift of the Holy Spirit. The promise is for you and your children and for all who are far off-for all whom the Lord our God will call." Acts 2:38-39 (NIV)

There are ways to teach your child to depend on God while at public school. The scripture above explains very clearly the promise is for you and your children! Amazing! As your kids go into public school to fight the good fight, keep leaning on God's promises together. The Bible will lead you and your children to experiences like we are having every day! It takes practice and constant surrender to depend on God. Even as adults, we may struggle with this.

Teaching our children at a young age to apply scripture while they are away from us is helpful. The idea is for our children to practice living out their own faith and not just leaning on their parents' faith alone. Choosing for themselves, of course, is the goal. When they are away from us and experiencing the majority of others in the public-school setting and applying their own faith, they are growing their faith. In my experience, it's better for children because they don't have the same filters we do.

They are not guarded and are bold in their speech, good or bad. Jesus wants people to come to Him like children, and He speaks on this in the Bible. "He called a little child to him and placed the child among them. And he said, 'Truly I tell you, unless you change and become like little children, you will never enter the kingdom of heaven. Therefore, whoever takes the lowly position of this child is the greatest in the kingdom of heaven.'" Matthew 18:2-4 (NIV)

One of the ways we encourage our children to implement faith was going through and discussing God's promises through scriptures. There are many! One of our favorites has always been Joshua 1:9 (NIV) "Have I not commanded you? Be strong and courageous. Do not be afraid; do not be discouraged, for the Lord your God will be with you wherever you go." Another great one we discussed is Jeremiah 29:11 (NIV) "'For I know the plans I have for you,' declares the Lord, 'plans to prosper you and not to harm you, plans to give you hope and a future.'" We explain to them how God is with them at school and how they can ask for help as we do daily. In the mornings, right before going into school, I would remind them to lean on God throughout the day and ask for help anytime they needed it. It could be with a friend, a test, or when they felt anxious about anything. The stories that came from this simple task were amazing! The looks on their faces showed it was growing their faith. For example, my middle child struggles with taking tests, and one day she asked God to help her remember what she had studied because her mind went blank. He helped her! She was very excited because she did well on the test! She came home so happy, saying that she asked for help and God answered her! This still happens frequently!

On another occasion, my oldest was in the second grade. We went on our after school walk to talk about her day. She told me she was playing on the playground with her friends at school, and a boy began being mean to her friends. She was a little afraid but decided to take up for them. She walked over to him and in a matter-of-fact way told him he didn't get here by himself, and he should get to know Jesus as his friend so he could learn how to be kind to people! Then she told him he needed to say he was sorry for being mean to her friends, which he quickly did! I was proud of her and asked her if this boy was in her class. She said, "No mama, he is a fifth grader." I was speechless! Talk about David and Goliath! I was so surprised at this story but what made it even sweeter, the boy asked her later who Jesus was. She shared her faith once again with this boy.

I'm so encouraged when I read my Bible! I love how God uses people who do not seem qualified. He pursues them, loves them, and wants to fulfill His purposes through us, all the while fulfilling our completeness in Him. Also, all the ways that God uses young children for His purposes amazes me! If you are wondering if you are qualified to lead your little children to face experiences head on, you are! I'm a witness to this, even though I didn't believe it at first. As you lean on God, step by step, He will show you and your little ones as he did mine. It's the truth. Our children belong to God before they belong to us, and who can love them better or more complete than He can? Love from God is not the same as love in the world. The love of God is unconditional and never changes. He is love. Children are a gift! The Bible says to "train up a child in the way he should go, and when he is old, he will not depart from it." Proverbs 22:6 (NKJV)

Every time our family has faced something hard in public school, God showed up after we prayed and asked for help. God directed us through scripture and used people, sometimes, in confirming our path forward. We listened and He led us through. He didn't make situations go away, though He could, but instead showed us the way through. How else are we to overcome if not to go through difficult things? How else is God to bring us and our children through if we don't show them where to lean for victories, comfort, guidance, healing, and so much more? Life is not easy! Don't we know it!

The children who are around our children in public school are watching how they respond to different things and what gets them through days that are full of joy and the days that are difficult. Problems are real. Children went through one of the hardest years ever experienced when the world shut down due to the Covid virus. We are seeing real problems with children now who do not have a safe place to go outside the home. They were isolated. We were all isolated and struggling! The ramification of that time is mind boggling.

Whether you are a believer or not yet, God created us for community. Humanity suffered during that time and there were lives lost for so many families, some from Covid, others to suicide, or other disease. How do we move forward in a way that helps our communities? We can reach out to our fellow neighbors to check in on them. We can show kindness to people as we go about our daily lives and smile at people we interact with. We can show concern for others in obvious need and actively help in some way. Too many kids in public schools are especially in need of these acts. We can encourage our children as they go into school and challenge them to do acts of kindness that would make a difference in another child's life. First, we need to care about others. We can act out love. The way we can do that better is to get to know Jesus by inviting Him into your heart and let Him change your life, your child's life.

Step one, receive Jesus. The Bible says, "If you declare with your mouth, 'Jesus is Lord,' and believe in your heart that God raised him from the dead, you will be saved." Romans 10:9 (NIV) If you have not done this yet and want a relationship with Jesus today, there is a simple prayer you can say: "Lord Jesus, I know that I am a sinner, and I ask your forgiveness. I believe you died for my sins and rose from the dead. I turn from my sins and invite you to come into my heart and life. I want to trust and follow You as my Lord and Savior. In Your Name, amen." Step two, read your Bible. If you are new to the faith, I would begin by reading the gospels: Matthew, Mark, Luke, and John. There are many different versions of the Bible. I have always loved The Message or The Living Bible. Step three, get plugged into a church that is based on scripture from the Bible. A few things to look for is that a church that accepts that Jesus is the Incarnate Son of God; they believe the Word of God is infallible; and we are all sinners saved by grace. God will lead you and help you! He helps me and my children every day. I don't have all the answers, but I know the One to lean on through it all. God, the One who suffered the loss of His son, Jesus on a cross to save all of humanity because He loves humans that much. He created us all for a purpose and because He wanted a family! Jesus is our helper. He sent the Holy Spirit to be our guide in life so we could actively live life how God intended. Jesus understood the impossible mission before Him. He chose death on a cross and rose to life on the third day and it was all about the solution for us to be able to have a relationship with God Himself. It was because of love.

LOVE:

"For God so loved the world that He gave his one and only Son, that whoever believes in him shall not perish but have eternal life." John 3:16 (NIV)

Jesus said to him, "I am the way, the truth, and the life. No one comes to the Father except through Me." John 14:6 (NKJV)

"If you love Me, keep my commandments. And I will pray to the Father, and He will give you another Helper, that may abide with you forever-the Spirit of truth, whom the world cannot receive, because it neither sees Him nor knows Him; but you know Him, for He dwells with you and will be in you. I will not leave you orphans; I will come to you." John 14:15-18 (NKJV)

CHAPTER 5
TEACH THE FAITH

Hear, O Israel: The Lord our God, the Lord is one. Love the Lord your God with all your heart and with all your soul and with all your strength. These commandments that I give you today are to be on your hearts. Impress them on your children. Talk about them when you sit at home and when you walk along the road, when you lie down and when you get up. Deuteronomy 6:4-7 (NIV)

Scriptures continuously guide us on how to teach our children. We are to "impress upon our children how to love God with all our heart and soul and with all our strength." Wow! How do we do that exactly? Communication and guidance; in addition, we should be in practice ourselves and thinking of ways to include our children in learning how God wants us to fight the good fight of faith together as families. I underestimated my children being able to handle situations when they were little, and I underestimated God's ability to guide them in those situations. God proved me wrong and showed me a different perspective by allowing me to see what was really happening. Victories with God were taking place. I was witnessing my children's faith growing stronger and stronger while fighting the good fight of faith in public school! The majority of children in the public school system have needs that we might not know about, but God does, and He is showing our children how to help, by sharing their faith.

Our daily communication with your child is important. In our busy schedules, you can still find moments to find out about their day at school. One of the ways we have interacted with our kids has been coming together each night for dinner. If that is not possible, it can still be done on the go. We have had many of our conversations in the car. One of the questions we would ask was what their favorite part of the day was. What was their worst part of the day? This will allow for finding out more detailed responses; sometimes the best stories of friends are during lunch or recess. Listening as they share is one of the best ways to be involved and show how much you care about them.

We, as parents, have bad days and good days. Children have them too. We always try to come together and invite Jesus into those moments, the good and the bad, so we can fully love on our child. Our family memorized a simple scripture to recite: "I can do all this through him who gives me strength." Philippians 4:13 (NIV) This scripture builds confidence to know that God is with you. I've seen it give my children strength in moments of need. No one wants to suffer, nor do we want our children to suffer in any way, but what I have learned in these many years of watching my kids go through hard things is that we cannot prevent this from happening.

I've also learned during my daily Bible reading that there are so many scriptures of promises to lean on in all circumstances. Here is a scripture about suffering: "Not only so, but we also glory in our sufferings, because we know that suffering produces perseverance; perseverance, character; and character, hope. And hope does not put us to shame, because God's love has been poured out into our hearts through the Holy Spirit, who has been given to us." Romans 5:3-5 (NIV) This is what suffering produces as we boast in the hope of the glory of God. I have witnessed this in my own life, and I see evidence in my children as well. Their growth in the Lord is unstoppable!

Did you know that many of the people in the Bible that God used for His purposes were children, not adults? I was reminded of this in my reading, and I was amazed how many times this occurred.

"Don't let anyone look down on you because you are young, but set an example for the believers in speech, in conduct, in love, in faith and in purity." 1 Timothy 4:12 (NIV)

Jesus said, "Let the little children come to me, and do not hinder them, for the kingdom of heaven belongs to such as these." Matthew 19:14 (NIV)

This is good news! You are never too young to follow Jesus and be a good example for everyone around you!

I remember one time when the kids were visiting their grandmother and my youngest was maybe four years old at the time. My mother-in-law suffers from fibromyalgia and has experienced a lot of pain in her legs throughout her life. She was having this pain during their visit, and I was told that my four-year-old laid hands on her legs, closed his eyes and prayed asking God to heal her pain. My mother-in-law shared this story with tears in her eyes and how it helped her in her faith. I remember how it impacted me as well. I was elated. Knowing that my youngest was acting on what he was learning, already impacting others. I was surprised, and it helped me in my faith.

When our kids were little, I remember always feeling like I was never doing enough as a mom. I constantly thought of everything I should be doing. Then I would get overwhelmed and not do anything, completely shutting down. I condemned myself all too often, never giving myself any grace. I would read my Bible and pray for God's direction every day because I wanted to be the best mom and not mess anything up! I knew I needed His guidance every day, so I applied the scripture I was learning. I would try to gather my kids in the mornings before school to pray, but it was chaos, with all three running every direction and me chasing them with diapers. Is it possible to laugh and be frustrated at the same time? I finally had a moment of clarity, choosing to do one thing: prayer in the mornings on the way to school to drop off my oldest. They were locked in their car seats and could not run! It wasn't such a big idea, but it helped us and brought some peace and calmness to the beginning of our day. It wasn't until later that year I implemented praying Psalms 91, having my oldest read it. Praying that scripture every morning changed everything!

After praying that scripture, we added prayer for their teachers and all teachers in Rutherford County. As some years passed, and they were making new friends, we began to pray for the friends they met who were struggling with difficult things like being hungry and homeless. Our kids would ask for extra food to put in their lunch boxes so they could share with that friend. We checked in on them to make sure they knew about the free food programs offered in public schools. I believe during this time; God was making us aware of others' circumstances. We are so thankful for programs like these that provide food for those in need! Our kids learned at a very young age how to love others and show acts of kindness.

We discussed simple things to do when there is a new kid at school: introduce yourself and have a conversation with them. We also discussed tangible ways to do things or say as they went to school daily, reminding them to look for the hurting, lonely, and isolated kids.

We also gave them different scenarios, acting out how to say something kind, ask how he or she is doing, introduce yourself, or ask to pray with them because it lets them know you care. You may be surprised how often each of my kids has done this and how often the child was receptive. There is a need for love here, and we can show our kids how to do this until they practice so often, it becomes a natural response. Learning empathy is so important. I've seen this grow in our children more and more as they continue to share their faith with friends and teachers in public school.

As our kids got older, they implemented their faith often, coming home with so many God stories! Making someone smile or letting them know you care is crucial. I remember how important it was for me as a child who was always the new kid somewhere and how much it meant to me to make connections with others who showed me kindness.

My husband and I discussed another thing that we introduced as our kids got older. When they would tell us about a circumstance or ask us what to do in a situation, we would put the question back on them and ask, "What do you think is their angle, or what do you think you should do? It seems simple but sometimes it can be hard to relinquish control on. We want to guide them and help them in every situation and tell them how to handle things that come up, but we also want a balance of teaching them how to be confident in their choices and lean into God for help with every need. The Holy Spirit helps us with all things. We can trust him! There's another scripture we lean on so we can gain strength and be safe. This scripture answers how we can be prepared and live this in public places that are especially difficult to navigate like public school. It is a good reminder that it's not people we need to guard against, it's spiritual darkness and Satan's tricks. God wants a relationship with all people, no matter their sin, God can meet anyone where they are!

> *"Last of all I want to remind you that your strength must come from the Lord's mighty power within you. Put on all of God's armor so that you will be able to stand safe against all strategies and tricks of Satan. For we are not fighting against people made of flesh and blood, but against persons without bodies- the evil rulers of the unseen world, those mighty satanic beings and great evil princes of darkness who rule this world; and against huge numbers of wicked spirits in the spirit world. So use every piece of God's armor to resist the enemy whenever he attacks, and when it is all over, you will still be standing up. But to do this, you will need the strong belt of truth and the breastplate of God's approval. Wear shoes that are able to speed you on as you preach the Good News of peace with God. In every battle you will need faith as your shield to stop the fiery arrows aimed at you by Satan. And you will need the helmet of salvation and the sword of the Spirit- which is the Word of God. Pray all the time.*

> *Ask God for anything in line with the Holy*
> *Spirit's wishes. Plead with him, reminding*
> *him of your needs, and keep praying*
> *earnestly for all Christians everywhere."*
> *Ephesians 6:10-18 (TLB)*

A fun way to communicate with your child is to go on one-on-one dates with them as often as you can. Making time for this is vital! It shows them how special they are when you plan things together to do their favorite things. My youngest child likes to watch a favorite show with me or sit on our front porch to talk. My middle child loves to hike and be in the woods. My oldest likes to go out to eat together and have long talks. All of these situations allow time to talk about what is going on in their world of school and friends.

In addition, learning your child's love language is one of the most important things. *The 5 Love Languages of Children* written by Gary Chapman helped me understand my child's needs more fully. The five love languages are quality time, physical touch, words of affirmation, acts of service, and gifts. Children need all five of these, but we noticed a top two as our kids got older. We recognized little ways to incorporate meeting these needs to fill their love tank. When their love tank is low, they act out in distress because they want your attention. If you are quality time and your child is acts of service, spending time together is great, but they may need an action in service to them that would help them feel more loved. I sewed a hole in my middle child's shirt, whose top love language is acts of service, and you would have thought I gave her a million dollars! Learning about people's love languages is important in all relationships, not just your children.

CHAPTER 6
BEING SALT AND LIGHT

"You are the light of the world. A town built on a hill cannot be hidden. Neither do people light a lamp and put it under a bowl. Instead, they put it on its stand, and it gives light to everyone in the house. In the same way, let your light shine before others, so that they may see your good deeds and glorify your Father in heaven."
Matthew 5:14-16 (NIV)

We are the light of the world! What a huge statement! What does this mean exactly, and how are we supposed to do what this scripture is saying? I relate this scripture to us because we are fighting the good fight of faith in a place that holds a majority of children from all walks of life. This scripture mentions a town, and it seems to be telling us not to hide our light. It's clearly stated for us to "let your light shine before others, so that they (the outside world) may see your good deeds and glorify your Father in heaven."

I am often reminded of a story that happened while my youngest was in 4ᵗʰ grade at the time. He got in the car after school that day, and we were on our way home. After asking each of our children what the worst part of their day was, we discussed their favorite part of the day. My youngest stated his favorite was playground time. I asked him why; did you get to spend time with your friends? He answered, "Yes, it was really fun." Then he continued sounding shocked and said, "Do you know none of my friends know who Jesus is?"

Our conversation:

Me: Did you talk to them about Jesus?

My child: Yeah, I told them how Jesus helps me, and they all asked who Jesus was, so I told them.

Me: There's many that don't know Him. That is so good that you got that opportunity to tell them! What happened after you told them?

My child: I told them if they want a relationship with Jesus too, they could get to know Him, and He would be with them. I asked them if they wanted to repeat a prayer with me to receive Jesus in their hearts, and they all said, yes, so we prayed and learned who Jesus was today.

Me: How many of your friends said this prayer with you?

My child: Seven.

I was so surprised, and I think I said back to him, "seven?" I wanted to believe I heard clearly. He continued to share Jesus with his friends that year. Our family celebrated that moment and gave all glory to God for the opportunity. God continued to present opportunities like this with the children that entered our lives and is continuing to do this daily every year. There are so many stories, and we want to share as many as we can so it can help other families or encourage and bring hope to those who share in these relatable experiences.

Another time, when our oldest was in the eighth grade, she made friends with the girls on the volleyball team at school and had a great year practicing and playing games that year. One of the girls leaned on her many times with her struggles she was having at home. Her troubles were so severe, she showed up at school one morning drunk with a thermos full of vodka that she tried to share with the people around her. This was a very hard situation to explain to my oldest child at the time. We prayed for her friend and had a conversation about how her friend was trying to numb her pain with alcohol. Her friend got sent home that day, the very place she was trying to escape.

I have a library at home where I keep extra books that have helped me through my journey. My kids have read them, and when they ask for one to share with a friend at school who is struggling, they are there to give it away. We have a box of Bibles in the back of my car for the same reason. We can't save all the children around us, but God can! Later, my oldest asked for a book in my library that covers rejection, a topic to which everyone can relate. *God's Remedy for Rejection* written by Derek Prince helped me address some of my past on this topic. It is universal pain that we have all experienced at some point. She gave that book to her friend who was struggling, and her friend read it. Afterwards, she wrote a long letter to my oldest expressing how much that book helped her and how she has never had a friend care about her so much. Her friend wanted to make changes in her life after that. One person showing that they care gave her strength.

When my middle child was in the eighth grade, there was a boy in class who sat beside her every day. They became friends. She said he was really quiet and didn't talk much, but he was really nice. As the year progressed, they talked more and more. One day, she noticed him crying and asked him if he was okay. He shared that his dad was mean, and they didn't have a good relationship. He also shared his dad was abusive. They talked for a while, and she asked him if he knew Jesus. He said he wanted to know Him, but he didn't know how. She told him he needed a Bible so he could learn how much Jesus loves him. He said he would get one. My middle child came home that day and told me what happened and asked if she could give him a Bible the next day at school. When she saw him, she asked if he bought one already. He said he asked his dad to take him to buy one, and his dad said no. When she reached in her backpack and gave him a

Bible, he looked so surprised and thanked her multiple times! They had more conversations about Jesus that year, and he became a Christian!

Praise God! He is our helper, and we are thankful for the opportunities every day. There are so many scriptures of God's promises that can encourage you in your journey. Don't give up! The Bible says, "Let us not become weary in doing good, for at the proper time we will reap a harvest if we do not give up." Galatians 6:9 (NIV)

There are many children in public schools that need Jesus, and they see that bright light in our children. The promise in Galatians is not just for us; it's for our children as well. We can encourage them by reminding them they have a purpose every day and to be aware of their surroundings.

God is helping us and our children! By learning how to stand where God wants you, you are teaching your child to do the same. It is important for your child to learn how to respond in every situation at every age. God is building their character now and giving them opportunities. How can we be in the world and not conform to the patterns of this world? The Bible says, "Do not conform to the pattern of this world but be transformed by the renewing of your mind. Then you will be able to test and approve what God's will is - his good, pleasing, and perfect will." Romans 12:2 (NIV) Scripture is clear that it is possible to be in secular places and still be able to not conform to the pattern of what's surrounding us. At the end of Romans chapter 12 in verse 21, it says, "Do not be overcome by evil, but overcome evil with good." We can overcome evil! The devil has free reign over the earth, but I have good news, God wins! We can stand boldly with Jesus inside us leading the way! This requires reading our Bibles and constantly renewing our minds so stand strong knowing He is with us!

When our kids were younger and understood what it meant to receive Jesus and have a relationship with Him, they each decided on their own when they were ready. They also received the baptism of the Holy Spirit around the same time because I would pray in my prayer language every morning for a few minutes, and they wanted to know about why I did this. They would ask questions about this, and we would read the scripture in Acts and discuss the stories. They were little but understood enough that they wanted everything that God offered as precious gifts. We would pray a few minutes in the mornings at the same time in our prayer languages, and soon they would do it on their own.

CHAPTER 7
PRACTICE FIGHTING THE GOOD FIGHT

"Finally, brothers and sisters, whatever is true, whatever is noble, whatever is right, whatever is pure, whatever is lovely, whatever is admirable- if anything is excellent or praiseworthy-think about such things. Whatever you have learned or received or heard from me or seen in me-put into practice. And the God of peace will be with you."
Philippians 4:8-9 (NIV)

Once again, in relating this scripture to where we are in fighting the good fight of faith in public school, we are putting this scripture into practice every single day. The promise is the God of peace will be with us! I learned this scripture years ago, but every time I've read it through the years, it has shown me something different wherever I am in my journey. We applied this scripture when learning what was appropriate and what was not appropriate for our kids to watch or listen to. It narrows dramatically what is a yes or a clear no. While making these rules for our kids, one of the things that stuck with me from reading my Bible was the part where it says, "Whatever you have learned or received or heard from me or seen in me-put it into practice." This was huge for me because I could watch anything I wanted as a child with no boundaries.

I wish I could go back in time and not have watched some of the things I did because I still think about some of the scenes, whether it was horror or sexual. I hope to be learning new things in my journey until I leave this earth, and I was thankful I began to learn this when my kids were little. I did not know until I did, and then I was a fierce protector of my children's minds, what they read, watched, or listened to. Does this get difficult to maintain as they get older? Yes, definitely! We often heard how their friends could watch anything they wanted. Our response was always the same, "It is our responsibility to protect your minds and your hearts. We will answer to God for our choices." The Bible says, "Above all else, guard your heart, for everything you do flows from it." Proverbs 4:23 (NIV)

We were consistent with this, but I'm sure we failed at times. We are not perfect. Don't condemn yourself if your child is older, and you did not think of this. I'm a living testament that God can redeem all of your past! The main website we chose to preview something that helped with what we were implementing whether movie, video game, book, or series is pluggedin.com. If I still wasn't sure, I would watch it myself or read the book that was of interest and go from there. I think this is something that everyone should consider implementing, not only for adults but for our children as well. We are seeing the fruits of our labor, and it was labor! It is difficult when you feel pressured to capitulate, but our kids are choosing on their own now. I direct them to look up whatever it is they are asking to read or watch, and sometimes they have decided that it wasn't appropriate or what they thought it was.

My husband and I decided we were not going to be parents who say no all the time, and it was always a yes unless it was a very clear no. We picked our battles but ultimately the parent must be consistent. We explained to our kids that images and words stay with you forever. We depend on God in prayer and reading our Bibles to try to learn what is right and good. Not everything is right or good, and we are their guides; however, we can put those decisions on them as they get older so they can practice what is right for them. When they are older and adults, we pray they make the same choices for themselves. They will make mistakes. We all fail, but when you practice guarding what goes into your mind and your children's minds, the transforming and renewing of your mind begins to take place over impulse, then you will be able to test and approve what God's will is!

> *"For I know the plans I have for you,"*
> *declares the Lord, "plans to prosper you and*

> *not to harm you, plans to give you hope and a*
> *future." Jeremiah 29:11 (NIV)*

Many Christians know this scripture. It's one of our favorites of God's promises! We have declared this and spoken it out loud many times. It's a good reminder that God is for us, and He wants this for all who come to know Him. Some will choose to follow Jesus, and some will not, but if anyone encounters our family, our hope is that they will see His love shown through us and want to get to know Him.

We don't have to be anxious about anything, we can trust God to be our helper. I can tell you I've had many anxious moments with myself and my children. God knows we are human, and we are going to go through some difficult things in our lives, but He wants to be a part of it because He loves us and wants to care for us in a way that the world does not understand. When we open our hearts to Him and search for the Truth, He says we will find Him! When I'm anxious, I look for those scriptures that will help me. There are many to choose from, but I love the one in Philippians, "Do not be anxious about anything, but in every situation, by prayer and petition, with thanksgiving, present your request to God." Philippians 4:6 (NIV)

One of our favorite books to give away is a promise book. I love how it is sectioned out in categories like fear, love, salvation, anxiety, faith, etc. In those categories, there is scripture pertaining to whatever category you need at the moment or an easy way to memorize scripture to help you. One way we connected with teachers was giving these promise books to teachers at Christmas time along with a thank you note. Also, in the bag were homemade chocolate chip cookies! It was a way to connect with teachers. After Christmas break one year, we received a card from one of those teachers. She said she read through the fear chapter in the promise book we gifted her, and it really helped her because she struggles with fear. She also asked where she could find promise books so she could order some for her whole family!

Other ways to connect with teachers are field trip days, finding out their favorite drink or food from their favorite place, and randomly sending in a gift card for no reason. Just a simple note of appreciation is a huge way to express that you're thankful for them. Even if you don't think you have time, you can send a simple email just to thank them. It means so much! When they get to middle school and high school, it does get harder to reach out because they change classes and have so many teachers, but there are still ways to connect. Sometimes we can be quicker with the negative, and we ignore the ways we can add a kind action to their day. A thank you card or an email to each teacher would surely be a great act of kindness!

Since our children were little, we have prayed over what teachers they get every year. Even if they got a teacher that was harsh, we prayed through, and they overcame the circumstances. It was our hope that our children would learn how to deal with difficulties, because not everyone they will encounter will be kind. People have insecurities and project them sometimes in negative ways. They have their favorite teachers, and they are the ones they will remember forever! We are still connected and friends with the kindergarten teacher that two of my children had. I had so many great experiences with many of their teachers in elementary. The ladies that run the front office were so special to us, too!

I remember a really hard time when I learned my middle child had severe speech difficulty. We didn't know where to turn and didn't have much money for companies that specialized in speech therapy. After a while, I was desperate to reach out to all the people who might know how to help us. I was thankful for a contact from a family friend who told us our middle child met requirements to apply to a public-school speech program that was offered. Our middle child was in this program for five years and accomplished so much with so many sweet teachers loving on my child. I could see her confidence growing in her every year, and her victories were big! We were so proud of her for overcoming the hard moments, and I cannot express enough all the struggles to get to achieve! It was a lot of added work at home. She worked hard and never gave up. I am so thankful for the public school system to offer this help to families. I am thankful for the kindness of teachers that helped her be successful and believed in her and filled her with hope!

Teachers in public schools are our world's best! My dad and stepmom were educators and I saw the love and care they had for the kids and teachers in their school. To this day, they still have students they have helped reach out to them on social media to keep in touch. Teachers are some of the hardest workers I know, and they care so much about children and want every child to succeed. Are there some bad apples in the bunch? Sure. But it does not take away from the many that love their job and want to do their best for our kids.

Let's also be sure to mention and be thankful for other public-school workers such as administration, bus drivers, cafeteria workers, janitors, guidance counselors, speech therapists, dyslexia specialists, and special education. Also, all the aid workers that are placed in for extra help for children like for sign language for children who are deaf. My family and many other families would like to thank you for all of your hard work, and please know you are very appreciated! Please also know we pray for all of you and your families year-round!

CHAPTER 8
PARENTS LEAD

"Start children off on the way they should go, and
even when they are old they will not turn from it."
Proverbs 22:6 (NIV)

In order to train our child the way he/she should go,
we need to be in training ourselves by reading our Bible
and living it out! God wants a relationship with us!
Devotionals are a great way to begin your day. They have
daily encouragement and relatable stories connecting
scripture with our lives today. I like to read in the mornings
on my porch. My mind seems better to receive while I'm
having coffee in nature. Obviously, my days are super
busy like most people, but when I take initiative to do
something that brings an uplifting guidance to my day, I
want to do it. Sometimes, while I'm on my break at work,
I read if I didn't have time that morning. Depending on
your schedule, nights might work better for you. Either
way, planning ten or fifteen minutes, we can all do

it! Our kids will see the priorities you have and how you spend your time. Let's be a good example for them, or they will turn to the world for that example. We are the difference makers and can teach them to be as well, not by conversation only, but by our example and actions.

> *"For where your treasure is, there your heart*
> *will be also." Matthew 6:21 (NIV)*

Our kids pay attention to things we do and how we respond to every circumstance. Living by example is important. Parents are only human and will make mistakes. This isn't about being perfect or pretending to do nothing wrong. As their caregiver, sharing with our kids and being vulnerable as we learn is so important because they are smart and can see the situation for what it is. I cannot tell you how many times I've apologized to my kids for the way I handled something or raised my voice out of frustration. I would go to them separately and say I'm sorry and ask if they would forgive me. They were so little and quick to forgive me. When they fought as siblings when they were little, I would make them apologize to one another, and they each would have to ask for forgiveness and respond with, "I forgive you." Why did I do this with them? The Bible speaks on forgiveness many times, but one scripture stood out to me. "For if you forgive other people when they sin against you, your heavenly Father will also forgive you. But if you do not forgive others their sins, your Father will not forgive your sins." Matthew 6:14-15 (NKJV) I explained to them that forgiveness is a choice, not a feeling. We can release holding on to those feelings that would create bitterness and choose to forgive. It made a difference all those years ago to have done that with them because now I believe that's why they are able to say they are sorry more readily, acknowledging when they did something or said something wrong that caused hurt feelings.

I get so encouraged when I read my Bible! I love how God pursues people who feel they are not qualified and uses them. He wants to fulfill His purposes through us, all the while fulfilling our completeness in Him. Also, all of the ways God uses young children for His purposes amazes me! If you are wondering if you are qualified to lead your little children to face experiences head on, you are! I'm a witness to this, even though I didn't believe it at first. Who would have thought I could come out of the circumstances I lived through? I can tell you I believed I was the last one to be qualified to have a wonderful marriage and three beautiful children to raise!

I have learned in my journey that sometimes it's the very person that does not think they are qualified who is. As you lean on God, step by step, He will show you and your little ones as He did mine. It's the truth. Our children belong to God before they belong to us, and who can love them better or more than He can? Have you asked God to show you what your child's purpose is? Did you consider it may be a different plan than what you may have in your mind? Our daily decisions with our kids matter.

Maybe it was because of my past that I pondered these questions. It mattered to me what God would choose for my kids, because I knew nothing other than God can decide better than I can, and I wanted the best for their lives. I have seen how God has changed unimaginable things in my life, and I have learned how to trust Him. It didn't happen overnight. Trust has always been hard for me. What I learned as a child is that you should not trust anyone. They will hurt you. They will hit you. They will abandon you. They can appear to love you, but in the end, it's not the kind of love you wanted or would seek out. Knowing Jesus changes everything! I have learned over time God's goodness, and I can trust Him. I can teach my children they can trust Him, something I didn't find out until later in life. It's never too late to tell God you are ready for a relationship with Him! God will never abandon you! "Trust in the Lord with all your heart and lean not on your own understanding; In all your ways acknowledge Him, and He shall direct your paths." Proverbs 3:5-6 (NKJV)

Every single time our family has faced something difficult in fighting the good fight in public school, God showed up after we prayed and more importantly, we listened. He led us. One of the ways we did this was focusing on the solution instead of the problem.

For example, one of the worst years for my oldest was her fourth-grade year. The problem was she had a girl bullying her. It lasted almost the whole year. It was a day-by-day struggle. Some days, honestly many days, I wanted to give up and help her escape somehow. I saw her pain and wanted to make it go away. I know hard things come; we had to face what was happening and teach her how to navigate the situation. Running away was not the answer; teaching her how to respond was the answer. People who are mean or bullies are just insecure and hurting. What is the solution to this problem? This particular girl was in fourth grade and what could her life be like at home to act in this way? Bullies are everywhere. Some are children, and some are adults. How do I teach my children how to navigate these hard situations?

Step by step, day by day, we leaned on a solution: scripture. The Bible is a life book. We prayed for this girl every day that year, and I had to make frequent visits to the school because of this child's actions toward my child. On one occasion, the girl shoved my oldest when she was praying in the hallway with her friend who was upset and crying at the time. I went outside when I heard this happened so I could be alone, and I walked our tree line up and down. I was in tears while talking to God. At my worst moment, I was angry, and I cried out to God. I did not understand why this situation was not getting better and told God, enough already! Then I started sobbing again because I felt so weak and helpless at that moment. I could not make things better for her. As I stood there with the trees, my thoughts cleared and said, His power is made perfect in our weaknesses, God rewards those who diligently seek Him.

I knew that was from the Lord. I recognized that it was God's promises in scripture. In that moment, I gained strength to move forward. I ran inside and quickly shared what had just happened with my oldest, and we prayed together. It was not long after that things began to slowly happen that were clearly God moments. Teachers were approaching my oldest to tell her they were watching her the whole year, and they were so impressed by how she handled something that was so hard.

The students that saw her get shoved in the hallway while praying for her friend were applauding her strength. God helped her. He does not abandon His children! The girl that targeted my oldest wanted to be friends with her in the end because she saw a light in her that she wanted to have. I was proud that my child distanced herself from this girl while still responding with kindness and love. She also learned how to assert herself toward someone who was mistreating her. She learned how to overcome something that was difficult and leaned on God throughout the whole ordeal.

I witnessed my child's faith grow that year more than ever before. Toward the end of the school year, all three of my children were rewarded in different ways. Our two oldest got invited to be in special pictures made for the front office. They were also given plaques because of their behavior the whole year. On a separate occasion, our youngest was approached in the library by the SRO of the school and was given a badge because of his noticeably good behavior the whole year. He told my youngest he was a good example for others, and he was proud of him. When these things happen and they come home telling me all the good news, I stand in awe of God, time and time again, because of His goodness and guidance. He gets all the glory!

> *"Not only so, but we also glory in our sufferings, because we know that suffering produces perseverance; perseverance, character; and character, hope. And hope does not put us to shame, because God's love has been poured out into our hearts through the Holy Spirit, who has been given to us."*
> *Romans 5:3-5 (NIV)*

The Bible tells us how to be in relationship with one another and how to imitate Jesus in his humility, we are to learn from him and then act on it!

> *"Therefore if you have any encouragement from being united with Christ, if any comfort from his love, if any common sharing in the Spirit, if any tenderness and compassion, then make my joy complete by being like-minded, having the same love, being one in spirit and of one mind. Do nothing out of selfish ambition or vain conceit. Rather, in humility value others above yourselves, not looking to your own interests but each of you to the interests of the others. In your*

> *relationships with one another, have the same mindset as Christ Jesus: Who, being in very nature God, did not consider equality with God something to be used to his own advantage; rather, he made himself nothing by taking the very nature of a servant, being made in human likeness. And being found in appearance as a man, he humbled himself by becoming obedient to death-even death on a cross! Therefore God exalted him to the highest place and gave him the name that is above every name, that at the name of Jesus every knee should bow, in heaven and on earth and under the earth, and every tongue acknowledges that Jesus Christ is Lord, to the glory of God the Father." Philippians 2:1-11 (NIV)*

One of the many things I love about this scripture is how it teaches us how important other people are and how we are to value others above ourselves, not looking to our own interests. In my experiences, there is so much reward in this perspective. God values all people and wants us to be unified; however, first we have to understand the concept of having the same mindset as Jesus before we can learn how to fully love people His way. It's hard to know how to love people sometimes, especially those who make it difficult to love them. God calls us to love the unlovable. The Bible goes even further to say, "Love your enemies, do good to those who hate you, bless those who curse you, pray for those who mistreat you." Luke 6:27-28 (NIV)

1 Corinthians 13, often called the love chapter, tells us what real love is and what it should not be. We can teach our kids these scriptures, but how often do we act it out? How do we respond to someone who mistreats us, and how do we teach our kids about love and about people who will hate us? Life is hard and being a Christ follower is hard, and I believe our kids can be guided step by step how to respond in hard circumstances at any age. Being in a public school and learning how to fight the good fight of faith in this setting is not easy! If you are reading this and you have kids in public school, you already know that it is a battle, not only for good grades, but also the extreme pressures that come with these times.

No limits or boundaries on social media have left a trail of heartache for kids everywhere. Although social media has positive ways to communicate with friends and family, we are learning now what it has influenced and how badly it's being misused for bullying, trafficking, sexual behavior, predators, and so much more. Again, communication with your child, certain boundaries and protective apps can be put on phones where you can monitor everything. As a result, you can teach your child responsibility while protecting them from the dangers that come with having a phone. Being aware is a big part of knowing your child's needs and what they are dealing with day to day while fighting the good fight of faith. They are connecting with hundreds of other children in public school on a daily basis, and we can prepare our children with the tools they need to be themselves and show the kindness needed in our world today. Since God is the One who created kindness and teaches us His ways that lead to victories, we should give more attention to scripture and experience those victories that He wants to bring for us and His Kingdom.

CHAPTER 9
YOU ARE NEVER ALONE

"So do not fear, for I am with you; do not be dismayed, for I am your God. I will strengthen you and help you; I will uphold you with my righteous right hand." Isaiah 41:10 (NIV)

I have often felt alone at times through my whole life, and when I feel that way, I tend to isolate myself. In those moments, fears take over; I feel I have no control over my thoughts. Feeling alone is Satan's way of keeping us where he wants us: disengaged. Fear is crippling. Fear can keep us from being who we are and living our lives fully. Fear is mentioned hundreds of times in the Bible. God is constantly telling us in scripture to not be afraid- He will help us! It makes sense to tell us that many times because we are only human, and we are going to be afraid sometimes. Remaining in that fear, however, can cause chaos in our lives, depression, health problems, anxiety, irrational thoughts, and so much more. I am mentioning those things because I have experienced all of them. I have seen loved ones who have suffered from many of them. There is a response we can practice to battle against it. I realized the different fears I had were really because of my lack of trust in God. I still have fears that creep in all the time, but now I recognize I need to replace those lies that fill me with fear with God's truth in scripture. Here are a few more scriptures that help me and my children. It is helpful to memorize and recite them out loud, especially if you struggle daily.

"For those who are led by the Spirit of God are the children of God. The Spirit you received does not make you slaves, so that you live in fear again; rather, the Spirit you received brought about your adoption to sonship. And by him we cry, "Abba, Father." The Spirit himself testifies with our spirit that we are God's children." Romans 8:14-16 (NIV)

"For God has not given us a spirit of fear, but of power and of love and of a sound mind." 2 Timothy 1:7 (NKJV)

"Have I not commanded you? Be strong and courageous. Do not be afraid; do not be discouraged, for the Lord your God will be with you wherever you go." Joshua 1:9 (NIV)

"We demolish arguments and every pretension that sets itself up against the knowledge of God, and we take captive every thought to

*make it obedient to Christ." 2 Corinthians
10:5 (NIV)*

God has plans for us and our children right now and in
the future. What are your hopes and dreams for your child?
Do we believe God wants the best for us and them? Right
now, my husband and I are teaching our children how to
fight the good fight of faith in public school. We practice
daily so they will know how to respond as they become
adults. It is our hope that they will be more knowledgeable
on how to respond to all people in the world because of
the practice and guidance they've had through reading
scriptures then applying and sharing their faith in a public
school.

> *"For I know the plans I have for you, says the
> Lord. They are plans for good and not for evil,
> to give you a future and a hope." Jeremiah
> 29:11 (TLB)*

> *"Guide me in your truth and teach me, for
> you are God my Savior, and my hope is in you
> all day long." Psalms 25:5 (NIV)*

When my kids were little and beginning public school,
I remember thinking we were the only Christians there,
even though it wasn't true. There are others fighting the
good fight of faith in public schools across Rutherford
County and beyond. We learned that when I wrote my
six weeks' study and brought the local public-school
families together in a community setting. Each time

we are gathering over the years, we are gaining strength from each other to know how to move forward with the changing system of public schools. Things that we face in public schools are ever-changing, and it helps to gather with people who understand what we are up against on a daily basis.

> *"Fight the good fight of faith. Take hold of the eternal life to which you were called when you made your good confession in the presence of many witnesses."*
> *1 Timothy 6:12 (NIV)*

How many stories from the Bible can you think of where God uses one person and brings victory against something much bigger? There are so many! Esther, David, Elijah, Samuel, Josiah, Elizabeth, John, Mary, Abraham, Moses, Rahab, and so many others! The list goes on and on! We are not alone! We all have a purpose, and God will lead His people through every circumstance we face and bring victories like we've never seen before. Some of the ones I mentioned from the Bible stories were young children and changed a nation. Although we do not know exact ages in some, others we do. Josiah, for example, became a king at eight years old. The Bible says God was pleased with Josiah for doing what was right. God used Josiah's life to save a nation! He reigned as a king in Jerusalem for thirty-one years! Esther is another young person of the Bible. She saved the Jewish people by gathering courage in her circumstances and standing up for her people when she could have easily been killed!

I wonder what our world would look like if we all took our place in our purpose for God with no fear but boldness in walking with Him in our world today. Our place is in public schools. It is not a popular place for a Christian person. In reading my Bible daily, I recognize that the young people God was using for His glory were in the middle of the masses, different varieties of people. It encourages me and should encourage you as well! If you are already standing and aware of helping your child in your particular public school, gathering other families whose experiences are similar will help you in fighting the good fight of faith. We can all be encouraging to each other while also praying for each other and our children. Attached at the end of this book is a six weeks' study for K-12 that I developed to bring our public-school community together and share different ways to navigate and encourage one another. It has helped hundreds of other families gather strength in handling the different situations that come our way in what our children are exposed to and how to bring victories, then spreading the Good News of what is happening far and wide! Gathering at your home, church, or other meeting place once a week for six weeks will guarantee encouragement and hope for you and all who come.

> *"Therefore, since we are surrounded by such a great cloud of witnesses, let us throw off everything that hinders and the*

> *sin that so easily entangles. And let us run*
> *with perseverance the race marked out for*
> *us, fixing our eyes on Jesus, the pioneer*
> *and perfecter of our faith. For the joy set*
> *before him he endured the cross, scorning*
> *its shame, and sat down at the right hand*
> *of the throne of God. Consider him who*
> *endured such opposition from sinners, so*
> *that you will not grow weary and lose heart."*
> *Hebrews 12:1-3 (NIV)*

If we can have the perspective together when looking at the teachers and students in public school as people who may not know God yet and need to know about Him, that's really when we can go in together with a mission that everyone is worthy of God's love. God cares about the institution of public school. He cares about all people and wants us all to come to know Him. When we care more about others above ourselves and we share our faith to the masses, Jesus can take over and do what He does: save.

> *"They defeated him (the devil) by the blood*
> *of the Lamb and by their testimony; for they*
> *did not love their lives but laid them down for*
> *him." Revelation 12:11 (TLB)*

The Bible tells us in 2 Timothy 4 to preach the Word of God, to endure hardships in season and out of season, being watchful in all things, doing the work of an evangelist, fulfilling our ministry. There are many places in the Bible that talk about enduring hardships. Every single story in the Bible is about enduring hardships and overcoming those hardships! Obviously, public school is definitely a place to endure hardships; however, in walking with the Lord for many years and learning scripture, I have learned in my experiences and my kids' experiences that serving God His way has never been the easy path to take. Whether or not you are in public schools because you chose it, or you didn't have any other option, I hope this book helps you to know you are not alone! For all of us, I hope after all the enduring and victories of overcoming, we can stand together with our children by our side and say together, "I have fought the good fight, I have finished the race, I have kept the faith." 2 Timothy 4:7 (NIV)

Remember the gladiator? When he went into the arena, he had to be actively ready with his weapons to fight. He faced opposition. He may not win every single fight, even with the preparation and training. Or maybe he does win every fight when you consider another perspective: the audience. We don't know what each of them is thinking while they watch the gladiator in the arena. Maybe they want to be a strong gladiator someday: maybe they don't think they have what it takes to be accepted as a gladiator. The gladiator brings hope for the audience. Win or lose, maybe the gladiator brings hope to the audience. Hope is everything. In the same way the audience is looking at the gladiator, other children and teachers are looking at our families as we navigate the arena of public school. An audience is always watching and paying close attention to the faith we have. God is God over all. He is in control. We are the instruments that God uses to further His Kingdom. We can trust Him. He never fails. In the arena of public school, we can all be gladiators for God and experience countless victories!

CHAPTER 10
HOW IT ALL BEGAN

The urgency to help other families in public schools began in my heart several years ago. My husband and I prayed all the time because we were filled with hope of what was happening with our family, and we wanted to share that hope to encourage other families that were in other public schools throughout Rutherford County.

In the spring of 2014, I was leading a mom's group at my church. I led the group every Wednesday for a number of years. As I was welcoming the moms, all of a sudden, I heard a voice very clearly inside my head that said, "You will not be here much longer." God was speaking to me! Although I was shaken, I still had to lead my group through the topic that morning. I kept thinking; *did God really speak to me audibly?* This had never happened to me before, but I knew it was Him. Eventually, I came to believe He meant for me to take on a new role. I did not understand, but I was obedient anyway, and I finished that summer leading one last study with my group. During that summer, I was filled with an unexplainable urgency to continue meeting with ladies outside of church who had children in public school. We would discuss our experiences in public school, and I was able to share about how God was moving through my children. They were so amazed by my stories. I was exhilarated to spread the hope we were experiencing. God was doing unbelievable things!

The scriptures that would come to my mind more and more heavily were the ones that direct us to spread the good news of Jesus! I continued to wait on the Lord to direct me with what was next for me. I prayed a lot during this time: It was really difficult. I was waiting on God to understand what my next step should be. We continued to spread the good news to other families who had children in public school. It did not begin as a mission. As time went by, more and more things were happening that were clearly unexplainable and could only be God. God continued to speak to me through scriptures He would bring to my mind.

> *"Go into all the world and preach the gospel to all creation." Mark 16:15 (NIV)*

> *"Therefore go and make disciples of all nations, baptizing them in the name of the Father and of the Son and of the Holy Spirit, and teaching them to obey everything I have commanded you. And surely I am with you always, to the very end of the age." Matthew 28:19-20 (NIV)*

When I read scripture, I strive for understanding. Scripture is there for us to contemplate what God wants as we learn and grow in our relationship. When we are consistent with our relationship, God unfolds the mysteries within the stories of the Bible to us and meets us where we are in our journey. He shows us our path when we seek Him. At first, I imagined the preceding scripture meant to be a missionary traveling to other countries. I didn't understand the magnitude of the situations in public schools until we were there and having the experience. God continued to give our family better knowledge of the dire circumstances every year: at that time, it became our mission.

One day, my heart was so heavy thinking about the help that was needed for the children we were trying to help in public school. I cried so hard and could barely pray out loud to God. Finally, through my tears, I cried out, "There is a need for more help in public schools to spread the gospel! We feel alone in this mission!" I heard in my thoughts, "the harvest is plentiful and the workers are few." I had read this scripture plenty of times before, but I needed to look up where it was, so I had an understanding of what God was trying to show me. I was so surprised as I read the whole context.

> *"Jesus went through all the towns and villages, teaching in their synagogues, proclaiming the good news of the kingdom, and healing every disease and sickness. When he saw the*

> *crowds, he had compassion on them, because*
> *they were harassed and helpless, like sheep*
> *without a shepherd. Then he said to his*
> *disciples, "The harvest is plentiful and the*
> *workers are few. Ask the Lord of the harvest,*
> *therefore, to send out workers into his harvest*
> *field." Matthew 9:35-38 (NIV)*

God showed me in that moment Jesus had compassion on the crowds because they were helpless, like sheep without a shepherd. I was feeling the same compassion for many of the families in public school! God gives us solutions in scripture. After a clear understanding was made known to me, I explained to my husband and our children. We then began to pray together nightly and ask the Lord of the harvest to send out more workers to public schools everywhere!

> *"Even the youths shall faint and be weary,*
> *and the young men shall utterly fall, but*
> *those who wait on the Lord shall renew their*
> *strength; They shall mount up like eagles,*
> *they shall run and not be weary, they shall*
> *walk and not faint." Isaiah 40:30-31 (NKJV)*

Months passed. I met with a couple of friends often, and I vented to them how I felt called to help families, and I did not know what was to be my next step. They were very supportive. One friend said I should write something. Anyone close to me knows I love to write, but I still wondered how my writing would bring families together. Then one day, I was walking with my friend, and she said I should write a study. Immediately, I was filled with joy. I did not know how I would get the information out there for what I was doing, but I just trusted the Lord and started writing. As soon as I sat down, each title for each chapter came to my mind. There were six, including the title of the study:

Fighting the Good Fight of Faith With Your Child in Public School.

The study took a few months to write, but I wrote the six weeks' study, complete with scriptures, questions, and a prayer at the end. I used scriptures that we leaned on in our family. The questions that accompanied the scripture were to help lead people in discussions of how we can navigate together with our children in public schools having a biblical worldview. In thinking further about what this study could do for families, I knew I needed my husband to lead with me. God completely guided the whole process!

I didn't have social media at that time, so it would definitely be God moving if we found enough people to bring together for the study. I was worried about this, but again, I trusted God that this study I would write would help families. God answered so many prayers during this time; I was overwhelmed with joy.

My husband and I began our first time leading the six weeks' study at our home with some friends. I was so nervous but excited for the opportunities ahead! Through the following years, we continued to lead many groups, and it spread by word of mouth. I would also meet families while volunteering at the school or on field trips, and that led to opportunities to invite them to our study. Later, our pastor approved our study to be able to lead a small group in our church instead of our home. I also had the wonderful opportunity to put our study in the bulletin at our church. Because of that, the study reached families that I could not have reached! I am so thankful for those moments, and my husband and I have stayed in contact with so many people who have attended our study over the years. We are stronger than before! Gathering together as a community because we're experiencing the same arena of public school, made us stronger!

Over the years of leading, *Fighting the Good Fight of Faith with Your Child in Public School*, there was an urgency in my heart to reach more people, so they could be encouraged in their personal sphere of people they know. I thought long and hard. My husband and I prayed. There were only two of us: my husband and me. The idea came that anyone with a child in public school could lead my six weeks' study at their home, in their neighborhood, with their friends, or in their church. God is so good! I began handing out my study whenever I would speak with a group of families in public schools. I would also randomly give them to people I would meet if they were interested. My husband would give the study to dads he worked with and would encourage them to lead a group with people they know. At this time, there is so much interest! We are so encouraged about how many families the study is helping! Now other people are leading, not us! The opportunities are growing beyond what I even dreamed. The hope is spreading! For families who want to navigate public school with a Christian worldview, there isn't anything available that substantially helps. This study will help you and encourage you. I am continuously grateful for how God leads our family! He gives us the tools we need to spread hope and encouragement to others. We are not alone!

I invite you to become part of God's Gladiators of faith! All things are possible with God. Utilize scripture and encourage one another. Your story with your children could be more magnificent than our story. You have a purpose. Don't underestimate the faith that exists in your children. They have a purpose, and it does not matter their age! They are the difference makers that can reach the hearts of many other children. Build their foundation with God at home and send them out each day, armed with the tools they need to share Jesus with everyone! The world is full of hurting and broken people. The arena that we are in together has a majority of children who have a variety of different circumstances. Communicate and talk with your children how to love others as Jesus does. Yes, it's that simple.

> *"Truly I tell you, if you have faith as small as a mustard seed, you can say to this*

mountain, 'Move from here to there,' and it will move. Nothing will be impossible for you." Matthew 17:20 (NIV)

Now, go move that mountain!

BASICS ON HOW TO LEAD A STUDY

1. The group size should be no more than twelve people so it can be a more intimate setting and not overwhelming. Smaller may be better to allow everyone to have time to input their thoughts or experiences.

2. Invite neighbors, friends, or anyone in your sphere of influence that have children in public school.

3. The group can meet in your home, at church, a playground, or any meeting place that allows for privacy. A babysitter may be needed for children. If there is an older child in the group gathering that can watch the other children in a bonus room or area that allows for playtime or a movie, that could work well too. Ask your group how they would like to address childcare if there is a need.

4. Begin the study with introductions, then a fun ice breaker. (Example: Where is your favorite place to go on vacation as a family, favorite hobby?)

5. Start with a prayer before you begin study then launch into the study questions. Each chapter of study includes scriptures. I usually begin by going around letting each person read the scriptures out loud first, so it is fresh on the mind.

6. Each question is designed to bring different thoughts or ideas. Give each person time to answer.

7. Plan to end the study each time in 90 minutes.

Sometimes it will end a little early or a little later depending on how much time is spent on questions. Everyone can pray the prayer at the end together out loud before dismissing group.

THOUGHTS FOR LEADERS

1. Don't let gathering for a study to be stressful! It should be fun!

2. Greet everyone with a smile!

3. There is no pressure to have food or drinks. The preference is yours to choose. Make it simple and welcome people with tea or coffee.

4. Someone in the group may be the main talker and that is okay. Guide as you can and don't be afraid to intervene with a thought you have to regain conversation that has gone off topic. Everyone should be able to have the chance to speak.

5. Sometimes people are quiet and that is okay. During the moments after initially asking a question, sometimes people are thinking and need a minute.

6. Ask if there is anyone that has any input or experiences they would like to add before moving on to the next question. This is a setting to share ideas with each other! There are so many perspectives we could learn so we can implement new ideas to navigate public school better than before.

7. Everyone can lead a study, including you! You are qualified to bring people together!

FIGHTING THE GOOD FIGHT OF FAITH WITH YOUR CHILD IN PUBLIC SCHOOL

Session 1-Prayer Changes Everything

Psalms 91 (NKJV)

[1] He who dwells in the secret place of the Most High
Shall abide under the shadow of the Almighty.
[2] I will say of the LORD, "He is my refuge and my fortress;
My God, in Him I will trust."

[3] Surely He shall deliver you from the snare of the fowler
And from the perilous pestilence.
[4] He shall cover you with His feathers,
And under His wings you shall take refuge;
His truth shall be your shield and buckler.
[5] You shall not be afraid of the terror by night,
Nor of the arrow that flies by day,
[6] Nor of the pestilence that walks in darkness,
Nor of the destruction that lays waste at noonday.

[7] A thousand may fall at your side,
And ten thousand at your right hand;
But it shall not come near you.
[8] Only with your eyes shall you look,
And see the reward of the wicked.

[9] Because you have made the LORD, who is my refuge,
Even the Most High, your dwelling place,

¹⁰ No evil shall befall you,
Nor shall any plague come near your dwelling;
¹¹ For He shall give His angels charge over you,
To keep you in all your ways.
¹² In their hands they shall bear you up,
Lest you dash your foot against a stone.
¹³ You shall tread upon the lion and the cobra,
The young lion and the serpent you shall trample
underfoot.

¹⁴ "Because he has set his love upon Me, therefore I will
deliver him;
I will set him on high, because he has known My name.
¹⁵ He shall call upon Me, and I will answer him;
I will be with him in trouble;
I will deliver him and honor him.
¹⁶ With long life I will satisfy him,
And show him My salvation."

Psalms 100 (NIV)

A psalm for giving grateful praise.

¹ Shout for joy to the LORD, all the earth. ² Worship
the LORD with gladness; come before him with joyful
songs. ³ Know that the LORD is God. It is he who
made us, and we are his. We are his people, the sheep
of his pasture. ⁴ Enter his gates with thanksgiving
and his courts with praise; give thanks to him and
praise his name. ⁵ For the LORD is good and his love
endures forever; his faithfulness continues through all
generations.

1 Thessalonians 5:16-18 (TLB)

[16] Always be joyful. [17] Always keep on praying. [18] No matter what happens, always be thankful, for this is God's will for you who belong to Christ Jesus.

Proverbs 3:5-6 (NIV)

[5] Trust in the LORD with all your heart and lean not on your own understanding. [6] In all your ways submit to him, and he will make your paths straight.

Hebrews 12:2 (TLB)

[2] Keep your eyes on Jesus, our leader and instructor. He was willing to die a shameful death on the cross because of the joy he knew would be his afterwards; and now he sits in the place of honor by the throne of God.

Matthew 6:31-34 (NIV)

[31] So do not worry, saying, 'What shall we eat?' or 'What shall we drink?' or 'What shall we wear?' [32] For the pagans run after all these things, and your heavenly Father knows that you need them. [33] But seek first his kingdom and his righteousness, and all these things will be given to you as well. [34] Therefore do not worry about tomorrow, for tomorrow will worry about itself. Each day has enough trouble of its own.

Session 1- Questions

1. Is prayer a priority in your life? If so, how? Before school, what do your mornings look like?

2. In what ways could you incorporate prayer time with your child in the mornings to start your day? Also, after school time?

3. How could you encourage your child to pray with others at school?

4. Read Matthew 6:31-34, Do you worry about your child while he/she is at school? If so, name some ways you can trust God more and worry less?

Prayer:

Heavenly Father, thank you for your loving guidance in my life. I yield to your wisdom and authority for my life. Today I am choosing to make prayer a priority in my daily walk with you. I want to be closer to You than ever before. I need you. My child needs you. Continue to lead me on Your path to righteousness. Thank you for being my Helper. In Jesus's name, amen.

FIGHTING THE GOOD FIGHT OF FAITH WITH YOUR CHILD IN PUBLIC SCHOOL

Session 2-Ways to Teach Your Child to Depend on God at School

Matthew 28:19-20 (NIV)

[19] Therefore go and make disciples of all nations, baptizing them in the name of the Father and of the Son and of the Holy Spirit, [20] and teaching them to obey everything I have commanded you. And surely I am with you always, to the very end of the age."

Psalms 62:5-8 (TLB)

[5] But I stand silently before the Lord, waiting for him to rescue me. For salvation comes from him alone. [6] Yes, he alone is my Rock, my rescuer, defense, and fortress—why then should I be tense with fear when troubles come? [7] My protection and success come from God alone. He is my refuge, a Rock where no enemy can reach me. [8] 0 my people, trust him all the time. Nur out your longings before him, for he can help!

Psalms 18:12 (TLB)

[2] The Lord is my fort where I can enter and be safe; no one can follow me in and slay me. He is a rugged mountain where I hide; he is my Savior, a rock where

none can reach me, and a tower of safety. He is my shield; He is like the strong horn of a mighty fighting bull.

Isaiah 30:21 (TLB)

[21] And if you leave God's paths and go astray, you will hear a voice behind you say, "No, this is the way; walk here."

Acts 2:38-39 (NIV)

[38] Peter replied, "Repent and be baptized, every one of you, in the name of Jesus Christ for the forgiveness of your sins. And you will receive the gift of the Holy Spirit. [39] The promise is for you and your children and for all who are far off—for all whom the Lord our God will call."

Isaiah 41:13 (TLB)

[13] 1 am holding you by your right hand—I, the Lord your God—and I say to you, don't be afraid; I am here to help you.

Session 2-Questions

1. It takes practice and constant surrender to depend on God. What questions can we ask our child to get him/her thinking about leaning on God at school?

2. The Holy Spirit is our Helper. How can we, as parents, encourage our child to pray when they need help at school?

3. Have you had prayers answered when you have prayed for your child at school? If so, how has it grown your faith? Has your child shared with you how God has helped him/her during school?

4. In Acts 2, Peter tells about the gift of the Holy Spirit. Who is the promise for? Do you believe your child, whatever the age, can receive this promise?

5. Your very special child has a purpose that God has for him/her. What is your role in helping your child to find his/her purpose?

6. As believers, we should be teaching our child to be a disciple for Jesus. The light of Jesus shines so bright and children have their way of sharing their faith in ways we may not think of. How do you believe it will influence other children in their school?

Prayer:

Heavenly Father, thank you for the promises of your Word! I praise you and ask for the boldness I will need to stand where you want me in my walk with you. I choose to fix my eyes on Jesus! May you give me the courage and strength I need to be your disciple every day! In Jesus's name, amen.

FIGHTING THE GOOD FIGHT WITH YOUR CHILD IN PUBLIC SCHOOL

Session 3-Connecting with Your Child to Find Out About Their Days in School

Galatians 5:22-26 (TLB)

²² But when the Holy Spirit controls our lives he will produce this kind of fruit in us: love, joy, peace, patience, kindness, goodness, faithfulness, ²³ gentleness and self-control; and here there is no conflict with Jewish laws. ²⁴ Those who belong to Christ have nailed their natural evil desires to his cross and crucified them there. ²⁵ If we are living now by the Holy Spirit's power, let us follow the Holy Spirit's leading in every part of our lives, ²⁶ Then we won't need to look for honors and popularity, which lead to jealousy and hard feelings,

Romans 5:3-5 (NIV)

³ Not only so, but we also glory in our sufferings, because we know that suffering produces perseverance; ⁴ perseverance, character; and character, hope. ⁵ And hope does not put us to shame, because God's love has been poured out into our hearts through the Holy Spirit, who has been given to us.

Philippians 4:13 (NIV)

[13] I can do all this through him who gives me strength.

Matthew 19:14 (NIV)

[14] Jesus said, "Let the little children come to me, and do not hinder them, for the kingdom of heaven belongs to such as these."

1 Timothy 4:12 (NIV)

[12] Don't let anyone look down on you because you are young, but set an example for the believers in speech, in conduct, in love, in faith and in purity.

Ephesians 6:1-3 (NIV)

[6] Children, obey your parents in the Lord, for this is right. [2] "Honor your father and mother" which is the first commandment with a promise [3] "so that it may go well with you and that you may enjoy a long life on the earth.

Ephesians 6:10-18 (TLB)

[10] Last of all I want to remind you that your strength must come from the Lord's mighty power within you. [11] Put on all of God's armor so that you will be able to stand safe against all strategies and tricks of Satan. [12] For we are not fighting against people made of flesh and blood, but against persons without bodies—the evil rulers of the unseen world, those mighty satanic beings and great evil princes of darkness who rule this world;

and against huge numbers of wicked spirits in the spirit world.

[13] So use every piece of God's armor to resist the enemy whenever he attacks, and when it is all over, you will still be standing up.

[14] But to do this, you will need the strong belt of truth and the breastplate of God's approval.

[15] Wear shoes that are able to speed you on as you preach the Good News of peace with God. [16] In every battle you will need faith as your shield to stop the fiery arrows aimed at you by Satan. [17] And you will need the helmet of salvation and the sword of the Spirit—which is the Word of God.

[18] Pray all the time. Ask God for anything in line with the Holy Spirit's wishes. Plead with him, reminding him of your needs, and keep praying earnestly for all Christians everywhere.

Session 3-Questions

1. Our daily communication with our child is important. In what ways can we communicate with our child about their day at school?

2. Read Philippians 4:13. We, as parents, have bad days and good days. Our child has them too. How can we invite Jesus into the good moments and the bad to fully love on our child? Who can we depend on to give us the strength we need in those moments?

3. It is easy to feel defeated when your child is struggling. If you tend to focus on the problem your child is struggling with instead of a solution, how can we lean on God's promises and shift that perspective?

4. What are some ways you could encourage your child to persevere through hard situations at school? Read Romans 5:3-5. What does it say will happen when they persevere?

5. Read I Timothy 4:12. This is good news! You are never too young to follow Jesus and be a good example for everyone around you! Do you believe your child could set an example in school? Is he/she already being a good example? If so, share a story of this.

6. Read Ephesians 6:10-18. Why does the scripture tell us we need to put on all of God's armor? Why is this important to do? Should we discuss this scripture with our child? Why?

Prayer:

Heavenly Father, thank you for helping me with all things in my life! Thank you for being with my child while they are at school and helping them with their needs. Please continue to guide me so I can connect with my child the way You need me to as their parent. You are Sovereign! Thank you for watching over us. In Jesus's name, amen.

FIGHTING THE GOOD FIGHT OF FAITH WITH YOUR CHILD IN PUBLIC SCHOOL

Session 4-Ways to be Involved at School with Teachers/Child's Friends

Philippians 4:8-9 (NIV)

[8] Finally, brothers and sisters, whatever is true, whatever is noble, whatever is right, whatever is pure, whatever is lovely, whatever is admirable—if anything is excellent or praiseworthy—think about such things. [9] Whatever you have learned or received or heard from me or seen in me—put it into practice. And the God of peace will be with you.

Matthew 5:14-16 (N1V)

[14] "You are the light of the world. A town built on a hill cannot be hidden. [15] Neither do people light a lamp and put it under a bowl. Instead, they put it on its stand, and it gives light to everyone in the house. [16]1n the same way, let your light shine before others, that they may see your good deeds and glorify your Father in heaven.

Galatians 6:9-10 (NIV)

[9] Let us not become weary in doing good, for at the proper time we will reap a harvest if we   do not give up. [1°] Therefore, as we have the opportunity, let us do

good to all people, especially to those who belong to the family of believers.

Psalms 55:22 (NIV)

[22] Cast your cares on the LORD and he will sustain you. He will never let the righteous be shaken.

Isaiah 41:10 (NIV)

[10] So do not fear, for I am with you;

do not be dismayed, for I am your God.

I will strengthen you and help you;

I will uphold you with my righteous right hand.

John 6:35 (NIV)

[35] Then Jesus declared, "I am the bread of life. Whoever comes to me will never go hungry, and whoever believes in me will never be thirsty.

Session 4-Questions

1. Whether you are a stay-at-home mom or dad, or you are working full time, there are many ways to connect with your child's teacher. Name five things you could put into action right now to make that connection.

2. Read Philippians 4:8-9. What do you think the outcome would be if you put these thoughts and what you have learned into practice? Can we encourage our child to do the same? How? The God of peace will be with us!

3. Read Isaiah 41:10. What does this scripture say not to do? What does God promise?

4. Your prayers make a huge difference in schools! We have discussed praying with our child. Do you pray for teachers and other children at your child's school? Would this be something you could include in your morning prayer time with your child? Do you have a favorite scripture for prayer time? If so, what?

5. God gives our child opportunities at school. There are many children in schools who need Jesus, and they see that bright light in our child. The promise in Galatians 6 is not just for us, it's for our child as well. In what ways can we encourage our child to be aware of those opportunities that will come?

Prayer:

Heavenly Father, thank you for my child's teacher and friends. Thank you for the opportunities that you give me so that I can share the good news of Jesus! Give me boldness and courage to shine my light as bright as I can for You. Help me encourage my child to do the same. I choose to love the people around me, including teachers. Break down every fear that comes my way so that I may complete the purpose you have for me.
In Jesus's name, amen.

FIGHTING THE GOOD FIGHT OF FAITH WITH YOUR CHILD IN PUBLIC SCHOOL

Session 5- Be a Good Example

Proverbs 22:6 (NIV)

⁶ Start children off on the way they should go,

and even when they are old they will not turn from it.

Philippians 2:5-11 (NIV)

⁵ In your relationships with one another, have the same mindset as Christ Jesus:

⁶ Who, being in very nature God, did not consider equality with God something to be used to his own advantage. ⁷ Rather, he made himself nothing by taking the very nature-of a servant, being made in human likeness. ⁸ And being found in appearance as a man, he humbled himself by becoming obedient to death-even death on a cross. ⁹ Therefore God exalted him to the highest place and gave him the name that is above every name, ¹⁰ that at the name of Jesus every knee should bow, in heaven and on earth and under the earth, ¹¹ and every tongue acknowledges that Jesus Christ is Lord, to the glory of God the Father.

Romans 12:2 (NIV)

2 Do not conform to the pattern of this world but be transformed by the renewing of your mind. Then you will be able to test and approve what God's will is-his good, pleasing, and perfect will.

Psalms 119:11 (NIV)

11 I have hidden your word in my heart that I might not sin against you.

Matthew 6:21 (NIV)

21 For where your treasure is, there your heart will be also.

Hebrews 11:6 (NIV)

6 And without faith it is impossible to please God, because anyone who comes to him must   believe that he exists and that he rewards those who earnestly seek him

Philippians 4:6 (NIV)

6 Do not be anxious about anything, but in every situation, by prayer and petition, with thanksgiving, present your requests to God.

Psalms 100 (NIV)

A psalm for giving grateful praise.

1 Shout for joy to the LORD, all the earth. 2 Worship the LORD with gladness; come before him with joyful

songs. ³ Know that the LORD is God. It is he who made us, and we are his; we are his people, the sheep of his pasture. ⁴ Enter his gates with thanksgiving and his courts with praise. Give thanks to him and praise his name. ⁵ For the LORD is good and his love endures forever; his faithfulness continues through all generations.

Proverbs 3:5-6 (NIV)

⁵ Trust in the LORD with all your heart and lean not on your own understanding. ⁶ In all your ways submit to him, and he will make your paths straight.

Jeremiah 29:11 (NIV)

¹¹ For I know the plans I have for you," declares the LORD, "plans to prosper you and not to harm you, plans to give you hope and a future.

Session 5-Questions

1. In order to train up our child the way he/she should go, we need to be in training ourselves by reading our Bible daily and living it out! So, if you don't read your Bible daily, let's start together today! God wants a relationship with us! What are some ways we can take initiative in getting our daily Bible time in our busy days?

2. What are three things you hope your child sees in you? What are three things you see in your child that give you hope?

3. Read Philippians 4:6. How can we express being thankful to God in every circumstance in our life? How would that impact your child who is watching how you respond to everything?

4. Do you think your attitude, good or bad, affects your child? If so, how?

5. God is helping us and our children. By learning how to stand where God wants you, you are teaching your child as well. It is important for your child to learn how to respond in every situation at every age. God is building their character now and giving them opportunities. Let's be our child's number one fan! God is!

6. Read Romans 12:2. How can we be in the world, but not conform to the patterns of this world?

Prayer:

Heavenly Father, thank you for the path that you are leading me on. Show me Your Truth. I don't want to be anxious about anything, I choose today to trust you. I rejoice today that I can rest in the shadow of the Almighty. You are my refuge and my fortress. Thank you for the hope and future that you have planned for me and my family. In Jesus's name, amen.

FIGHTING THE GOOD FIGHT OF FAITH WITH YOUR CHILD IN PUBLIC SCHOOL

Session 6- Fears to Overcome. Learn the Truth. You are not Alone!

2 Timothy 4:7 (NIV)

⁷ I have fought the good fight, I have finished the race, I have kept the faith.

Joshua 1:9 (NIV)

⁹ Have I not commanded you? Be strong and courageous. Do not be afraid; do not be discouraged, for the LORD your God will be with you wherever you go."

Jeremiah 29:11 (TLB)

¹¹ For I know the plans I have for you, says the Lord. They are plans for good and not for evil, to give you a future and a hope,

Romans 8:14-16 (NIV)

¹⁴ For those who are led by the Spirit of God are the children of God. 15 The Spirit you received does not make you slaves, so that you live in fear again; rather, the Spirit you received brought about your adoption to sonship. And by him we cry, "Abba,-Father," 16 The Spirit himself testifies with our spirit that we are God's children.

Psalms 25:5 (NIV)

[5] Guide me in your truth and teach me, for you are God my Savior, and my hope is in you all day long.

2 Timothy 1:7 (NIV)

[7] For the Spirit God gave us does not make us timid, but gives us power, love and self-discipline.

1 Peter 5:6-7 (NIV)

[6] Humble yourselves, therefore, under God's mighty hand, that he may lift you up in due time. 7 Cast all your anxiety on him because he cares for you.

Revelation 12:11 (TLB)

[11] They defeated him by the blood of the Lamb and by their testimony; for they did not love their lives but laid them down for him.

1 Timothy 6:12 (NIV)

[12] Fight the good fight of the faith. Take hold of the eternal life to which you were called when you made your good confession in the presence of many witnesses.

Session 6-Questions

1. Read Jeremiah 29:11. What are your hopes and dreams for your child's future? Do you believe God wants the best for your child? For you?

2. We are fighting the good fight of faith together with our children in public school. We can run this race and keep the faith. How many stories from the Bible can you think of where God uses one person and brings victory against something much bigger?

3. When we put our faith into action, we are trusting God. How has your faith impacted people around you? How has your child's faith impacted people around him/her?

4. Read Psalms 25:5. God is Sovereign. He is faithful. We have a teacher who tells us the truth. We have a responsibility in sharing that truth with others as we learn it. That includes our children. Share different ways we can boldly tell the truth to the people around us, including our child.

5. What fears have you had in the past? Do you have fears now? If so, what are they?

6. Read 2 Timothy 1:7 if you struggle with fear. How can reading this truth change your perspective? Would it help you to replace those lies that give you fear with the truth?

Prayer:

Heavenly Father, give us a boldness to proclaim the truth about Jesus. Forgive us of our pride and thinking we can do everything ourselves without You. We need You Lord. Pour out your Spirit over us today and awaken us to listen and turn our hearts toward You. Deliver us from all fears! We choose to trust You and We choose to be overcomers. We praise You Father. Thank you for never leaving us alone! In Jesus's name, amen.

Printed in the USA
CPSIA information can be obtained
at www.ICGtesting.com
LVHW022059120923
757981LV00010B/891